CN00660958

UGANDA

THE PEARL OF AFRICA

UGANDA

THE PEARL OF AFRICA

Photographs by
PAUL JOYNSON-HICKS

Introduction by
SHAUN MANN

QUILLER PRESS
LONDON

For God
Mum and Dad, Emma, Rowena, Simon,
Sprout and Amy

Copyright © 1994 Paul Joynson–Hicks

First published 1994 by
Quiller Press Limited,
46 Lillie Road,
London SW6 1TN.

ISBN 1 870948 93 9

All rights reserved.
No part of this work may be reproduced by any means without
the prior written permission of the publishers.

Designed by Peter Dolton.
Produced by Book Production Consultants Plc, Cambridge.
Printed by Salingraf Industrias Graficas, Bilbao, Spain.
Colour reproduction by East Anglian Engraving, Norwich.

Contents

Acknowledgements

There are so many people who have helped produce this book in lots of different ways but I can only mention a few here, so thank you very much to everybody who contributed.

This wouldn't have been possible without my parents Gill and Crispin Brentford, their support both financially and morally has been unending and I'm deeply grateful.

Many thanks to Birte and Philip Barnard, who have been vital in the production of the book and very kind to me; David Kane, a good friend and also vital in the production of this book; Shaun Mann for his help and his great text; Lara Calthorpe who taught me about a lot of things; Nels Porter, a great person who is continuously encouraging and someone who put up with my moods with great patience; James 'Ten languages' Muruli who drove me all over the place brilliantly; Rob Fairer-Smith kindly coped with my panicked faxes to the UK; Emma J-H, Ro and Si Banks and Amy my siblings (and in-law!) they're constantly there for me and are great friends; many thanks to Liz and Thor at Buhoma for putting us up and letting us in!; Alexis Hefley, a constant support and a great friend; thanks to Justin Dourado at Kenya Airways; the Sheraton Hotel; Paul, Tracy and Debs at Sky Photographic Services Ltd.; Jonathan Topps at Fuji Photo Film Ltd.; Eric Ndugwa of Uganda Hotels; Birte at the I.B.C.; Frank of Uganda National Parks and to John Gibbons for his advice and sense of humour! Special thanks to Richard and Lindsay Ibreck for finding me 'Reg' and for so much excellent input, and many thanks to all my good friends in Uganda.

An extra special thanks to my publisher Jeremy Greenwood, who put up with a considerable amount in the production of the book and managed to stay sane, thanks.

The last thank you must go to Uganda — such a beautiful country in a thousand different ways.

Introduction

Winston Churchill wrote of Uganda: "The scenery is different, the vegetation is different, the climate is different, and, most of all, the people are different from anything elsewhere … in the whole range of Africa". The text and photographs in this book will endeavour to allow the reader a view into the Uganda of today which has all the qualities Churchill enthused over nearly a century ago.

Uganda is saturated in colour, the outstanding natural beauty of its people and its landscapes have always stirred inspiration in travellers and residents.

Parts of Uganda have changed very little in the last hundred years; the period of turmoil between 1967 and 1986 virtually ground all industrial and economic progress to a halt. This was an era when other countries in Africa were enjoying the fruits of international aid and their economies expanded as fast as their populations. Uganda has only just started to receive positive international attention and it has been slow and cautious in coming. The increasing confidence with which donor countries treat Uganda is a direct result of its current leadership, which has been so responsive in progressive policy making. There has been much to learn, for both the donors and the public and private communities in Uganda, from the results around the rest of the continent. Lessons have been learnt. The result has been fast and real progress has been made. In some cases, Uganda has started to set trends for other countries to follow, financial policies have got to grips with wildfire inflation and currency fluctuations. The government is allowing free expression and, through this, is unifying the Ugandan peoples.

Matters of constitution and restitution are a priority, which is creating a very positive forum for peace and stability.

Agriculture, forever the backbone of the Ugandan economy (it employs about 80% of the active population), is starting to contribute, to debt service, rather than debt. The massive sugar and textile industries of the 1960s are reviving, along with the large tea estates long neglected. The government controls on the coffee and cotton industry have been loosened to allow the farmer a larger market in which to sell his produce, and private exporters have been granted licences. Horticulture and floriculture are receiving increased investment as aircargo becomes a viable means of export.

The government has facilitated foreign investment with attractive incentives and streamlined import and export procedures. Many expelled Asians have returned to reclaim their properties and are reinvesting in a growing economy.

Tourism, the most sensitive of all industries to develop, is finally attracting investment and interest. Significant progress has been made in the redevelopment of infrastructure in the National Parks. The devastation of the animal populations that took place during the war years is beginning to be repaired through increased control and management. New areas of interest such as mountain gorillas and ecotourism are putting Uganda back on the East African tourist circuit. The Nile, a source of wonder and inspiration for thousands of years, cuts a verdant and often turbulent median south to north through the country. The Nile flows from Lake Victoria at what was Ripon Falls and into Lake Kyoga. Still the Victoria Nile, it cuts a raucous passage west across Karuma Falls and through the narrow pillars of Murchison Falls towards Lake Albert. Finally the Albert Nile meanders along a slow, wide corridor into Southern Sudan. To the far west of Uganda, on the Zaire border, the snow

covered Rwenzori Mountains (or Mountains of the Moon as Ptolemy called them) rise into almost permanent equatorial mists. The mountain slopes have their own strange successive worlds of vegetation, each with its own characteristic flora. In the extreme south-west are the Mufumbiro volcanoes, a chain of imposing cones that rise out of the lava plain of the western rift. The tropical hardwood rainforests of Western Uganda such as Maramagambo, Budongo and Bwindi evoke adventure and wonder.

Kampala, the modern capital, is the centre of most economic activity. It is steadily being rebuilt after systematic looting and destruction during the changes of government. The city infrastructure has been restored and new office towers, hotels, stadiums and shopping malls are appearing almost monthly. Entebbe, the former administrative capital, is still very picturesque, though rundown and neglected. The century old botanical gardens are being restored to their former splendour. The presence of the international airport at Entebbe will ensure its continued restoration; His Excellency the President still lives there too. Of the other towns around the country, Jinja, at the source

of the Nile, Mbarara, on the road west, Fort Portal, at the foot of the Rwenzoris, and Mbale on the eastern border are all showing promising signs of economic recovery. The apparent slow development and poverty of areas outside Kampala is a combined result of cautious investment and the relatively recent restoration of countrywide infrastructure. Tourism and increased commercial agriculture will gradually redress the balance, as they have elsewhere in Africa.

Uganda is rich with culture and artistic talent, Ugandans are lively actors and public speakers. Hardly a night passes without the rhythmic sounds of traditional dancing or, in Kampala, modern disco music. The overriding impression of Uganda is of its happy people. Hardship and war are not forgotten, but they are in the past, to be recalled in silent prayers and thoughts for absent friends.

THE HISTORY

There is a legend documented by John Hanning Speke of how Uganda got its name. Uganda was the name of a prodigious hunter who came from Unyoro. He was a poor man who hunted to feed his family and was so successful, that he was soon feeding all around. He was eventually named Kimera, the first King of Buganda.

Precolonial

There are four main ethnic groups in Uganda which all have different origins. By far the largest in number, the Bantus, who came from the west, include the tribes of Buganda, Banyankole, Basoga, Bakiga, Batoro, Banyoro, Banyaruanda, Bagisu, Bagwere and Bakonjo. The Nilotics, who came from the north,

include the Lango, Acholi, Alur, Padhola, Lulya and Jonam. The Nilo-Hamitics include the Teso, Karamojong, Kumam, Kakwa, Sedei, Pokot, Labwor and Tepeth and the Sudanics include the Lugbara, Madi and Lendu.

The pre-colonial history of these tribes is not well recorded, genealogy being the only method employed by the early settlers in the area. At the time of the first exploration of Uganda there were three main kingdoms, each ruled by a Monarch and laws and customs of their own. The kingdoms of Buganda, Kitara (sub-divided into Bunyoro and Toro) and Karagwe are all well documented by the early explorers. The general opinion is that these kingdoms originated around the sixteenth century, the land before that probably being occupied by Bushmen. The Bantus originated from the west coast of Africa, migrating along the Niger river, they occupied the northern, central and western parts of Uganda. The eastern part of Uganda, occupied some 250 years ago by the Nilo-Hamitic tribes never formed a kingdom because the people were nomadic and the area was not well suited to agriculture. The different tribes got their names either from their leaders or some peculiarity in their customs or origins. The Karamojong for instance (aikar–to stay; imojong–old men) – the tired old men who stayed behind.

The Explorers

Giovani Miani, an Italian working for the Egyptians, was the first European to set foot in what is now recognised as Uganda. He visited northern Uganda at Nimule and Moyo in March 1860. The Maltese slave and ivory trader Andrea de Bono also made excursions into Uganda in the 1860s. Between 1849 and

1855 several German missionaries with the Church Missionary Society sent reports back to Europe of 'great lakes and snowy mountains' some weeks' journey inland from the coast.

In 1857, John Hanning Speke and Richard Francis Burton began an African expedition that would lead to Speke's discovery of the southern shores of Lake Victoria and a return journey by Speke and James Augustus Grant in 1862 that would reveal the source of the Nile at Ripon Falls (the plaque to commemorate this is now buried beneath the Owen Falls Dam). Speke and Grant followed the Nile north, through the kingdoms of Buganda, Karagwe and Bunyoro.

These first encounters with Mutesa, Rumanika and Kamurasi, the respective kings, provide some of the most colourful early records of life and death in Uganda. Subsequently, research has shown that Mutesa was arguably the 30th King of Buganda, thus dating the kingdom to the early sixteenth century. The rituals and customs set by the royal families were often cruel; torture, live burial and mutilation were common practice. The value of human life was not very high. Mutesa demonstrated this during Speke's second audience; he ordered a court page to shoot someone in the outer court to demonstrate the effect of one of the rifles given to him by Speke.

The search for the source of the Nile by the early explorers was responsible for attracting interest, through their journals, in Uganda and her peoples. The journals of Burton, Speke, Grant, Samuel Baker, Dr. Georg Schweinfurth, Henry Morton Stanley and David Livingstone so captured the imagination of Europeans, that the decades spanning the end of the nineteenth and beginning of the twentieth centuries saw literally hundreds of travellers coming to Uganda. Of course, with them came the prospects of trade and consequently British colonial interest. In 1893, Sir Gerald Portal raised the Union Jack in Port Alice (now Entebbe) and claimed Her Majesty's Protectorate over the kingdom that stretched north to the westward flowing Victoria Nile, east to the town of Tororo and west to the Rwenzoris and Virungas.

Of all the explorers, Samuel Baker and his wife Florence, who discovered and named Lake Albert and Murchison Falls, did most to uncover Uganda for their European public. Baker was determined and thorough, rather than excessive, about his exploration. He funded himself, and as such was neither an empire builder nor a reformist. His books were immensely popular because they brought the hitherto mysterious and cannibalistic interior of 'Darkest Africa' out of the realms of fantasy and into an understandable, habitable country with colourful denizens.

The Governors of Equatoria

In 1869 two significant events contributed to the history of Uganda. The first was the opening of the Suez Canal which linked Africa to Europe and hence facilitated trade routes via the East African coast, rather than the more traditional way into Uganda from the north and west. The second was the appointment of Sir Samuel Baker as the first Governor of Equatoria. Both were initiated by Ismael Pasha, the Khedive of Egypt, who was eagerly trying to establish a great Muslim state from Alexandria to Lake Victoria; the length of the Nile.

Sir Samuel Baker returned briefly to Uganda in 1869 and 1871 while governor of the Equatorial Province of Egypt. The cessation of the trade in slaves and the

expansion of the Empire to the Great Lakes was the dual mandate from the Khedive who was anxious to please allies in Europe. Baker based himself in Gondonkoro (close to present day Juba), in Southern Sudan, because the Nile south of that point dispersed into marshland and he could not guarantee supplies and protection.

This period in Uganda's history is marked by the ascension to the throne of Bunyoro by Kabalega. He succeeded his father Kamurasi, and was to become a constant thorn in the flesh of the British and Egyptian imperialists (as well as his Bagandan brothers to the south).

General Gordon followed Baker as Governor of Equatoria (1873–79). He travelled the area extensively and was responsible for commissioning the 'complete exploration of the sources of the Nile'.

Gordon tried to establish a series of linking forts along the west bank of the Nile from Khartoum to Ripon Falls. His failure to do so was the result of Kabalega's constant refusal to prostrate his kingdom before the Egyptians and later the British. Gordon had used a 108 tonne steamer called the *Khedive* to transport men and supplies into Uganda. He got as far as Lake Albert and was blocked by Murchison and Karuma Falls. He managed to send a predatory force of 160 men to set up a garrison in Mengo, Mutesa's capital of Buganda, they were captured and only narrowly rescued from the Baganda. Gordon gave up and returned to Egypt rather dispirited.

The final period of Egyptian domination of Equatoria was under the governorship of Emin Pasha (or Dr. Edvard Schneitzer) between 1879 and 1889. Emin Pasha was a sensitive and intelligent man. He was energetic and enthusiastic and travelled throughout the province. He recorded valuable notes on the Banyoro and their customs, and for a time was on equitable terms with Kabalega. Equatoria was finally abandoned by Egypt in 1889 when communications were severed by the infamous Mahdist revolt, and Emin Pasha, left stranded in Uganda, was rescued rather reluctantly by Stanley. At around this period in history, a 'scramble' for African territories was initiated by a sudden realisation of their importance. Uganda was no exception. Stanley's rescue of Emin was in fact a thinly disguised attempt by Leopold II of Belgium to gain control of the Upper Nile Region. Conversely, Stanley was determined to secure Emin's loyalty for the British. Simultaneously, a German expedition led by Dr. Carl Peters was also on its way to rescue Emin Pasha. Emin had a firm following in Uganda and both the Germans and the British were anxious to secure his services.

Ironically, Emin decided to join the German effort in East Africa after Stanley delivered him safely to the coast.

Two personalities emerged from the scramble for the colony between Germany and Britain. The man chosen to lead the British effort was Frederick Dealtry Lugard, while the Germans placed their faith in Dr. Carl Peters. In 1890, a treaty was signed between Mwanga, the successor to Mutesa, and the Germans. Politics in Europe changed the situation only months later and Lugard forced a rather confused Mwanga into another treaty, granting protection to Buganda in return for jurisdictional rights for the Imperial British East Africa Company, Lugard's employers. The territorial rights in Uganda had been swopped with the Germans for Heligoland.

Missionaries and Religion in Precolonial Uganda

The Arab traders had brought Islam to Uganda. Slavery and bigamy, so prevalent in Bagandan culture, were condoned by the Muslims; this made it a very easy faith to relate to. The antithesis of these values presented themselves in the Christians who arrived from Europe condemning slavery and advocating monogamy. Most relevant to Uganda was the conflict between the Protestants, represented by the Church Missionary Society (C.M.S.) and the Roman Catholics represented by the French White Fathers. The protagonists in the 1880s in Uganda were Alexander Mackay of the C.M.S. and Pere Lourdel of the White Fathers. Though ardent rivals, the two men were forced into friendship because of steadily increasing hostility from Mutesa who, by the early 1880s, had become unpredictable and bloodthirsty. When Mutesa died in 1884 and

his son Mwanga succeeded him, a new hope was short lived. Mwanga, who was only 18 years old, distrusted the missionaries and all their followers. He was responsible for the torture and murder of thousands of Christians, among them Bishop Hannington. The murder of Hannington and his retinue sparked a full year of relentless killings. It was not until Lugard came to Mwanga's court that the Kabaka had other matters, more pressing, to consider.

British Protectorate to Independence

Gladstone's government officially announced that Uganda was to become a British Protectorate in 1894. Lugard was largely responsible for settling the religious wars between the now Muslim Mwanga and Christian Kabalega and safekeeping the territory until the British moved in and the IBEA Co. was dismantled. In 1899 Kabalega and Mwanga were captured and exiled to the Seychelles. Having disposed of the 'troublesome elements' the British administration proceeded to install their own, carefully selected, kings of Buganda, Bunyoro, Toro and Ankole. The Baganda were used as agents in effecting British rule, a policy of convenience that was to have far reaching consequences for the future peace and stability of Uganda. The Buganda Agreement of 1900 set the trend for 'indirect rule', whereby the British would rule through the Bagandan oligarchy while retaining a facade of traditional government, hence creating a framework of British controlled civil servants. The British kept the Baganda out of the military and police forces with the excuse that they were too short. Hints of proletariat discontent came to a head in 1945 and 1949 with riots in Buganda. The riots were directed against the ruling oligarchy as well as the

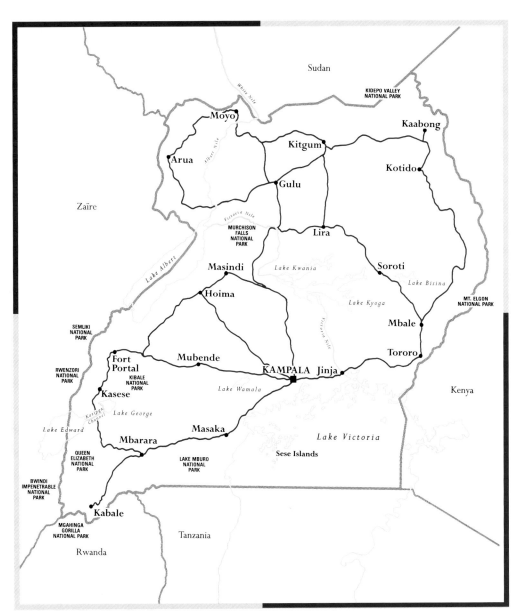

Sudan

KIDEPO VALLEY
NATIONAL PARK

Moyo

Kaabong

Kitgum

Arua

Kotido

Gulu

Zaïre

Lira

MURCHISON
FALLS
NATIONAL
PARK

Lake Kwania

Soroti

Lake Albert

Masindi

Lake Bisina

Lake Kyoga

Hoima

MT. ELGON
NATIONAL PARK

SEMLIKI
NATIONAL
PARK

Mbale

Mubende

Tororo

Fort
Portal

RWENZORI
NATIONAL
PARK

KIBALE
NATIONAL
PARK

KAMPALA Jinja

Kasese

Lake Wamala

Kenya

Lake George

Lake Edward

Masaka

Mbarara

Lake Victoria

QUEEN
ELIZABETH
NATIONAL
PARK

LAKE MBURO
NATIONAL
PARK

Sese Islands

BWINDI
IMPENETRABLE
NATIONAL
PARK

Kabale

MGAHINGA
GORILLA
NATIONAL PARK

Tanzania

Rwanda

party to be formed lead by a non-Bagandan was the Uganda Peoples Union (UPC); Apollo Milton Obote was its leader and became, on October 9th 1962, the first Prime Minister of an independent Uganda.

Post Independence Uganda

Because of loyal support in Buganda, when Obote formed his government, the KY was well represented (almost a junior partner in government). The Kabaka was elected Constitutional Head of State, while Obote ruled the country through his cabinet. Obote had inherited a promising country. The British had laid down all the necessary infrastructure for success. Makerere University and Mulago Hospital were well regarded institutions throughout the world, and industry, agriculture and trade were flourishing. On the other hand the melting pot of tribal, religious and political differences made the task of government very complex. The Independence Constitution was a difficult document to interpret having been written by diverse groups with self interest a prime motive. However, the fundamental stumbling block for Uganda's government was the anomaly between the alliance of the UPC and the KY. That Obote, a herdsboy from Lango, succeeded in implementing an alliance, and maintaining a friendship with the hereditary king of Buganda, was an outstanding political feat. The alliance was a means to an end; to prevent the DP from being re-elected after independence. Obote's own political ideologies were directed to creating a United Republic. He did this at the expense of the Bugandan Kingdom, expelling the Kabaka and abolishing the kingdom in the bloody massacre at the battle of Mengo in 1966. Kabaka Edward Mutesa II was forced into exile in England where he died in poverty three years

Asian and European monopoly in crop marketing and processing. The colonial structure of government was to remain in place with very little modification until Sir Andrew Cohen (Governor of Uganda, 1952–56) instigated a form of central government in 1953. In the same year, Kabaka (king) Mutesa II was deported to England for refusing to have any part in an East African Federation (he returned in 1955).

This event along with the formation of the Uganda National Congress (UNC), the Democratic Party (DP) and the Progressive Party, served to split the Bagandan hierarchy and further divide the country along religious lines. UNC was predominantly Protestant while DP had a Catholic executive committee. A traditionalist Bagandan party, Kabaka Yekka (KY) was formed as a direct result of Bagandan loyalty to the Kabaka. The first later. Obote abolished all other kingdoms and effectively alienated himself from most fractions of the population. All of this was done in the name of establishing "One Nation, One People, One Parliament" under Milton Obote.

The constitutional crisis in 1966 unearthed Major General Idi Amin, who was now at the head of an army Obote could not do without. Effectively, the military were the policy implementing body for a civilian administration. This situation prevailed until the 25th January 1971 when Amin ousted Obote, while Obote was at a conference in Singapore, and took over as Head of State and the military implemented their own policies.

The feeling throughout Uganda was one of relief and jubilation. The Baganda welcomed Amin to power with unrestrained enthusiasm. Amin maintained this momentum by returning the Kabaka's body to the Bagandans at the earliest opportunity. Worldwide, a new era was heralded for Uganda. The *Daily Telegraph* carried a front page picture of an unescorted Amin driving himself in an open jeep, unheard of for an African Head of State. Amin appointed an experienced and capable cabinet and pronounced a whole series of progressive reforms.

Killings in the army, where Amin's tribesmen were engaged in a systematic massacre of Acholi and Langi, were the first signs to a watching public of the madness to follow. The expulsion of the Israelis in 1972 was ultimately a result of their refusal to supply arms to Uganda. The Asian exodus was one of the most significant events in Uganda's history. It has scarred Uganda for the rest of its national life and the wound, only now beginning to heal, was open for nearly a quarter of a century. The reason for the

expulsion is not clear; certainly Amin was under significant internal pressure to 'deliver the goods' of post liberation euphoria and expectation, not just from the civilian population but also his army. The Asians owned and controlled over half the country's wealth and expelling them was a short cut to achieving what was expected.

In addition, Amin bore some motives for revenge on the British. Many Asians were British citizens and as he later put it when expelling the British, he "wanted to teach the British a lesson they would never forget". According to Amin, the reason for expelling the Asians was revealed to him in a dream, where God decreed that if he didn't do it, the country would be ruined.

Amin's last six years in power were marked with various failed coup attempts and continued threat of war from exiled Ugandans in Tanzania. The infamous "Raid on Entebbe" by the Israelis was a prominent news item in July 1976. Though Amin continued to exercise free licence to murder anybody he perceived to be a threat, people seemed to get on with life, albeit under fearful conditions. In 1978 he invaded Northern Tanzania in an effort to boost failing morale and wipe out more enemies. The retaliation was supported by many exiled Ugandan fighting troops, including the Front for National Salvation (FRONASA) which was lead by Yoweri Museveni. The advance on Kampala was swift against the demoralised, though heavily armed, troops of Idi Amin.

The Tanzanian and Ugandan liberators arrived in Kampala in April 1979 under the banner of the Uganda National Liberation Army (UNLA). Once again the chorus of jubilation echoed around the streets.

After a short period of indecision, the Uganda National Liberation Front (UNLF)

was formed from an amalgam of several Ugandan political and military groups. Not for the first time in Uganda's history the people had united against a common enemy. Once the dust settled, however, the all too obvious differences surfaced and the power vacuum could not be filled for long, if it ever was. Yusuf Lule was appointed President and remained in power for just two months. Godfrey Binaisa followed and was deposed in a military coup eleven months later. Paul Muwanga headed the Military Commission and announced that national elections would be held four months later, on the 30th September 1980. Once again Obote, who returned from exile, would contest elections as leader of the UPC. A third major political party emerged to do battle with the DP and UPC. It was the Uganda Patriotic Movement (UPM) and once more Yoweri Museveni's name was prominent in Ugandan affairs.

Milton Obote won the election with a comfortable, though dubiously attained margin and was sworn in as President on the 11th December 1980. Obote had an army under Major General Tito Okello firmly behind him and returned to power anxious for revenge on those who supported Amin in 1979. Worst of all for Ugandans, Obote had no control over the army, whose senior officers systematically plundered government coffers, and whose ranks looted and raped at whim.

Dissatisfied with the election results, Yoweri Museveni, together with 26 young men, retreated into the bush of the Luwero Triangle and started what was to be a long campaign of guerrilla warfare. The National Resistance Army (NRA) was formed under the banner of the National Resistance Movement (NRM).

The turning point in the long bush war

was the death of the UNLA commander, Oyite-Ojok, who was Obote's cousin. He was a powerful figure and his death demoralised Obote's troops and caused a power struggle within the Langi and Acholi factions of the army. Obote's men continued to run riot in the city and towns, frustrated at the lack of success against the NRA. Obote consistently resisted appeals to negotiate with the NRA and he gradually alienated the Acholi who felt they were fighting alone against the NRA. This lead to his final removal from power by his own army, for the second time.

The constitution was suspended, Parliament dissolved and Major General Tito Okello was sworn in as President in July 1985. The violence and lawlessness continued. Gradually the NRA gained more support and more control in crucial areas, while the Okello Government suffered at the hands of its free-riding army. Museveni and Okello met in Kenya and signed peace agreements for a new, equally represented government. Within a month of the agreement, it was obvious that both parties were not satisfied. The war intensified and the NRA moved closer to Kampala, the UNLA splintered and on the 26th January 1986 Kampala was overrun by the NRA.

Yoweri Kaguta Museveni was sworn in as President of Uganda on 29th January 1986. To a huge gathering outside the Parliamentary buildings, Museveni announced that his takeover represented a fundamental change in the affairs of Uganda and not a "mere change of guards". He proclaimed a ten point programme through which the NRM would "usher in a new and better future for the people of Uganda". The ten points included some issues ignored or maligned by the previous seven presidents, such as democracy, security, elimination of corruption and the

well-being of the economy of Uganda. To mixed reactions, a large, broad-based cabinet was appointed. It encompassed friend and foe alike. In an effort to unite every corner of Uganda under one government, Museveni included representatives of previously antagonistic political parties, tribal groups and religious factions in the government of the day. Museveni extended personal invitations to exiled Ugandans, to many he offered key government advisory or corporate positions. A significant 'brain drain' had taken place during the war years and Museveni was anxious that these individuals should return and help rebuild a fragmented and broken country.

When the NRA arrived in Kampala serious resistance was not encountered. The victorious soldiers were disciplined and friendly, the looting and uncontrolled killing of previous changes of leadership were absent. The army was within the law not above it.

The task that lay ahead in 1986 was immense. The distorted and violent policies of a whirlwind of governments had left Ugandans without a true belief in their leaders. Exposing a dormant National pride and identity was essential to rebuild the battered country and was always going to be one of Museveni's most painful and arduous tasks.

Convincing the people that a democracy would emerge from a military takeover and that measures such as the suspension of political party activities were for the common good did not auger well. The policy, however, was sound; it enabled everybody to settle down and take stock under the wing of the NRA. The country was in a mess and only a slow, systematic and transparent examination of the damage could begin to set wrongs to right.

The NRA re-established law and order everywhere in Uganda, except the north and north-east which remained bastions of discontent and insecurity. The sporadic lawlessness in the north has been a constant problem to the NRM, and until a National identity emerges the issue will remain.

Infrastructure in every aspect of life, whether the judicial system, the Constitution, roads, agriculture, health, education or tourism, had broken down. Infrastructural redevelopment was the starting point for the new government. In addition, a system of local government through locally elected officials was put in place from the very beginning. Every Ugandan is a member of at least one legislative body that gives him a voice in everyday affairs. This was to be the foundation on which National identity would be built.

The personification of Uganda's malaise has been the magnitude of the AIDS crisis. Uganda was one of the first countries in Africa to recognise and begin to deal with the problem. The results have been very positive. Education and awareness have been the key areas targeted by the programmes initiated.

With political stability and infrastructural redevelopment underway, the Government was able to focus on the ailing economy. Certain key issues such as the historical overdependence on coffee as a foreign exchange earner and the lack of a sound taxation policy were highlighted and measures emplaced to expedite change. With the liberalisation of the economy, foreign exchange is freely and legally traded over the counter. The coffee industry was also liberalised.

Internal change for the better has allowed the international image of Uganda to flourish. The achievements of the NRM and particularly Yoweri Museveni, are recognised and applauded outside Uganda. Museveni was elected Chairman of the Organisation of African Unity in 1990 and the following year was the first African leader invited to address the European Parliament in Strasbourg.

Foreign aid to Uganda has facilitated its recovery and foreign investment is now building on this. The NRM has taken longer than anticipated to achieve some of its goals, but they are being realised. With the help of every Ugandan, 'the Pearl' will once again shine in Africa.

GEOGRAPHY

The City and Towns

Kampala, or in the vernacular, 'the hill of the impala', is the old name for one of the hills on which the present capital stands. It is the site of Captain Lugards' original fort. Mengo, which was the Kabakas' residence, Rubaga, which was the hill of the White Fathers and Namirembe, the CMS Missionary hill and Old Kampala are the four hills always referred to in the writings of the early colonial administration. It was only later that the hills to the east of Old Kampala developed as the main civil, business and residential areas of modern Kampala. The city, as it is today, is recovering quickly from the ravages of war; Kampala is emerging from a cocoon of dilapidation and flourishing on the fruits and flowers of a stable and well supported government.

It was Sir Gerald Portal in 1894 who decided to administer Ugandan affairs from Entebbe because he found himself and his staff constantly besieged by 'petty day to day affairs' in Kampala. He felt the relative remoteness and tranquillity of Entebbe would

allow more work to be done. And so Entebbe (originally Port Alice, renamed by Portal after Ntebbe, the peninsular on which he built his home) became the civil administration seat of Uganda during the days of the Protectorate. Some government ministries still have their headquarters in Entebbe; most, however, have moved to Kampala. The main industrial town of Uganda is Jinja, it is the site of the source of the Nile and in the early days was a very significant trade route from the coast. It is the site of the Owen Falls Dam, which provides most of Uganda's electricity as well as being a centre for heavy industry.

The British were responsible for fortifying, and later placing colonial administration and infrastructure, in virtually every major town in Uganda. The development of towns such as Fort Portal, Hoima, Masindi, Mbarara, Kabale, Soroti, Gulu, Tororo and Jinja followed a very similar pattern throughout the country. A fort was built and sustained to keep law and order in the area, it was used as a base for local negotiations with hostile and friendly tribes; once the district was safe, civil administration was emplaced, followed shortly by public buildings such as court houses and administration blocks. Once a town was established it became a trading centre, once business was flowing, businessmen moved in – in the case of Uganda that was primarily the Indian and Pakistani 'settlers'. Shops, factories and warehouses were quickly erected and the towns were built up. The Protectorate administration took great pains to demarcate districts and their capitals according to existing ethnic boundaries. In the Bantu tribal areas this was a successful system, but in the north and east of the country, where ethnic groups were much more segmented, the shortcomings of the system were quickly exposed.

The towns and villages in the countryside are often very rundown; juxtaposed with the ruin and decay is fantastic backdrop scenery and spirited, happy people who have suffered and survived a very difficult generation.

Agriculture and Industry

Agriculture in Uganda is not an exact science. Most things grow in most places and it is an activity that has always been a part of rural life and one that has been the mainstay of the Ugandan economy with nearly 90% of the population being rural. Historically, not until the explorers, missionaries and eventually the British came to Uganda, was there any real trade in agricultural produce, certainly nothing was exported from Uganda until the early 1900s. Each kingdom had its own staple food source, whether bananas, cattle or millet; what they did not have was bartered from their neighbours. When the British began to administer Ugandan affairs, they realised the immense potential in Uganda for an export trade in agricultural commodities. Coffee and cotton were the early successes, later, tea, sugar and tobacco. All these industries suffered terribly during the war years through mismanagement, neglect and looting and pre-1970 export levels have not yet been achieved.

Robusta coffee is indigenous to Uganda; it had been cultivated by the Baganda for several hundred years before the first efforts to grow coffee for export in the early 1900s. Ironically, the first coffee to be exported from Uganda was of the arabica variety (imported from Malawi). Cotton was brought to Uganda by the missionaries; it was only grown commercially under the direction of the British who sent it all to India and later Egypt and Europe. Tea was brought to Uganda by the British and grown exclusively on large estates. The international market price for the traditional cash crops of coffee, tea, tobacco and cotton has fallen considerably relative to pre-1970s levels. This has led to a greater dependency on food crop production as a cash income which has in turn jeopardised the recovery of the coffee and cotton (traditionally smallholder based) industries as the rural farmers have reverted to food crops as a means of feeding and clothing their families. This divergence away from traditional cash crops has been good for Uganda's economy because farmers have been able to increase their income per capita with more efficient land-use and increased cultivation.

Non-traditional exports account for nearly a quarter of Uganda's export revenue from agriculture. They include: sesame seeds, fish and fish products, beans, maize, cattle hides and goat skins, soya beans, cocoa beans, timber, chillies, vanilla, millet, ground nuts, bananas and some spices. Horticulture and floriculture are fast emerging as future significant foreign exchange earners.

Industry in Uganda is expanding and diversifying rapidly. Food processing (including meat, grain milling, bakeries, sugar, coffee, tea, fish, dairy, animal feeds and oil milling) accounts for by far the largest sector of industrial activity. Timber, paper and printing, chemicals, paint and soap are other areas of recent rapid investment. Other steady industries such as steel and steel products, cement and brick production, tobacco and beverages, textiles and clothing and leather and footwear form the bulk of the remaining sectors of activity. The index of industrial production shows a steady increase since the present government took office, a sure indication of investor confidence.

The mining industry, around which the once highly prosperous town Kilembe was

built, is beginning once again to attract foreign investment. The resources are still in plenty and all the incentives and help that government can give are being given.

Tourism and National Parks

One could argue that John Hanning Speke was the first tourist in Uganda. In this day and age the concept of exploration definitely falls into the recreation category of our understanding. Winston Churchill was probably one of the earliest tourists, he arrived in Uganda by railway from Mombasa in 1907. Though the railway was completed in 1901, it was not until 1903 that it was fully operational. The railway brought tourists and East African Railways and Harbours took advantage of this by starting to run regular passenger trips on Lakes Victoria and Albert in fully equipped steamers. The journey from Butiaba, on Lake Albert, to Fajao, at the base of Murchison Falls, fascinated and thrilled every traveller that braved it. The banks of the river were teeming with animals. Churchill called the area "Kew Gardens and London Zoo combined on an unlimited scale".

Sadly, the animal populations suffered during the long years of war. National Parks were not regarded as sanctuaries by marauding or retreating armies, rather they were well stocked larders for hungry soldiers. The landscape, however, survived and so did the plethora of birdlife. Hotels and lodges, once the talk of East Africa, have fallen into disuse and dereliction. All the proud 'Uganda Hotels' are gradually being privatised in an attempt to encourage some foreign investment in a reviving industry. Reviving it certainly is. The original 3 National Parks, first declared in 1952, have expanded to 10 and efforts have been underway to re-establish and initiate suitable infrastructure to allow for

the anticipated influx of tourists. In addition, the government has made progress in freeing incoming visitors of cumbersome documentary requirements.

The National Parks in Uganda include:
    Queen Elizabeth National Park,
    Murchison Falls National Park,
    Rwenzori Mountain National Park,
    Bwindi Impenetrable National Park,
    Mgahinga Gorilla National Park,
    Lake Mburo National Park,
    Kidepo Valley National Park,
    Mount Elgon National Park,
    Kibale National Park
    and Semliki National Park.

Each park has its own unique features. Queen Elizabeth NP encompasses the Kazinga Channel between the twin lakes of Edward and George, as well as the tree climbing lions in the Ishasha sector reached through the spectacular Maramagambo Forest. Murchison Falls NP has the Falls and the inimitable River Nile. Rwenzori Mountains NP is the preserve of snow on the equator. Bwindi Impenetrable NP and Mgahinga NP are both mountain gorilla sanctuaries but have very different landscapes. Bwindi is a remarkable rainforest while Mgahinga NP straddles the enormous Virunga Volcanoes. Lake Mburo NP is the preserve of huge herds of zebra and other plains game. Kidepo Valley NP is remote and rugged, it is a small park and the animals are very easily seen. The area is arid and scenically unlike any other park in Uganda. Mount Elgon NP has an incredible range of flora and is a very popular hikers' destination. Kibale NP is rainforest reserve where the primary interest is habituated chimpanzees. Finally, Semliki NP is the home of the Pygmies and sulphurous hot springs. The Semliki river drains from the

Rwenzoris into Lake Albert through an immense tropical forest, home to many unique species of antelopes and primates.

The People

The present borders of Uganda, forged by the British between 1893 and 1926, encompass 28 major tribes divided into four main ethnic groups: Bantus, Nilotics, Nilo-Hamitics and Sudanics. The Bantu tribes, settled in particular districts in Uganda, tended to be pastoralists or agriculturists and had a central, politically organised government, often under hereditary kings. The non-Bantu tribes arrived in Uganda much later and, kept out of the already settled and more fertile areas, tended to have a more nomadic lifestyle with a loose, clan-based political organisation.

The Baganda are the largest ethnic group in Uganda, dominating the central region of the country, encompassing the districts of Kampala, Mpigi, Mukono, Masaka, Rakai, Mubende and Luwero. The Baganda have enjoyed and made good use of the opportunities afforded them by the British in the early days of 'indirect rule'; they are generally better educated and more wealthy than the rest of the tribes in Uganda. When explorers first came to Buganda, they found it an already well organised and prosperous society headed by a hereditary king or Kabaka whose power was absolute. A similar level of organisation was found further inland in the western region, where Bunyoro was another old kingdom ruled by their king, the Omukama. Today the Banyoro live mainly in the districts of Hoima, Masindi and Kibale. Still in the western region, but further south-west, towards the Rwenzoris, in the districts of Kabarole (Fort Portal) and Kasese, the Batoro people form another ancient royal kingdom under their Omukama. Together with the Banyankole from Mbarara and Bushenyi districts, who were also governed by a line of kings (Omugabe), these Bantu tribes were the most progressive in early Uganda. They were the early traders and, because of their organisation, were the focus of colonial activity and infrastructure.

Other Bantu tribes in the south-west include the Bakonjo and Bamba, who live mainly in the Rwenzoris and Kasese district, the Bakiga (hill people), who come from Kabale and Rukungiri districts and the Banyaruandak, who come from the Rwandese border district of Kisoro. In the eastern district and neighbours of the Baganda, are the Basoga from Jinja, Kamuli and Iganga districts. Further east, towards the Kenya border and Mount Elgon, the tribal areas are smaller yet equally well defined. Bukedi district is shared mainly by the Bagwe, Badama, Basamia, Banyuli and Bagwere. The Mount Elgon district of Bugisu is the home of the Bagisu (or Bamasaba) and the Highland Nilotic people called Sebei.

The three remaining ethnic groups occupy the northern, north-east and north-west regions of Uganda. The Karimojong, Iteso, Kumam, Sebei, Labwor and Dodoth are Nilo-Hamitic tribes occupying the north-east region including Kotido, Moroto and part of Soroti district. The various migrations of this group of peoples have been traced to a common origin in Abyssinia – the Karimojong were the first to settle, they were left behind by the Iteso who settled further south. The northern region of Uganda is occupied by the Nilotic Acholi in the north and the Langi in the south. The remaining Nilotic tribes occupying the north-west include the Alur, Japadhola and Jonam. Sharing the region are the Sudanic tribes of Lugbara, Madi, Okebu and Lendu. The settlement and segregation of these areas of northern Uganda is complex – most of the tribes were constantly shifting because of war, drought or disease and they had no system of government, each clan being more or less autonomous.

In addition (to the above peoples) there is a small tribe of transient pygmoids called the Bambuti that live in the forests along the Zaire border. They are few in number and are very shy, still preferring to live according to their old traditions.

Kampala

The clock tower roundabout on the southern side of Kampala.

Making cooking pans from old oil drums. Here, he is banging the cut out pieces into shape.

The finished product on sale at Owino Market in downtown Kampala. This is where most of the products from Kisenyi are sold.

Polishing pieces of jewelry made out of cattle horns.
One of the many small, yet innovative businesses around Kampala.
It produces items such as earrings, bangles, necklaces and rings.

A local carpenter at Katwe.

Lunch for all. This lady is preparing casava and sweet potatoes which she will sell to the workers in her area by the plate.

The Kasubi Tombs.

The Tombs were built by Mutesa I in 1882 on the site of a former palace. King Mutesa I of Buganda was the first king to be buried there. His three successors were also buried there.

The inside of the tomb.

Kasubi also serves as a cemetery for other members of the Royal Family of Buganda, who are buried outside the big house.

The Parliament Building.

Pouring purple dye onto seed stock kidney beans. This prevents the beans from being eaten or stolen.

The matatu park in downtown Kampala.

Concentration lapses at a primary school in Kampala.

Selling matoke early in the morning on Gaba Road.

The 18-hole golf course, being played under the gaze of the Sheraton Hotel.

FACING PAGE
A typical Kampala street vendor.

The Kampala
Sheraton.

Making prefabricated buildings at an Alam Group warehouse.

A pavement newspaper vendor.

Sesame seeds being hand sorted. This removes stones and detritus.
The seeds are then packed in sacks and resold to exporters or the local market
(for flour making and oil extraction). Sesame is rapidly becoming a very important
non-traditional export for Uganda.

Almost absolute concentration in this primary school.

Christophe and Godfrey are playing 'mweso', a type of African draughts.
Once some expertise is gained, this is a fast and exciting game.

Entebbe

Kampala Road, the main street of Entebbe. It was the administrative capital of Uganda until independence. Originally named Port Alice (after the first steel boat on the lake brought by the first CMS missionaries) Entebbe is one of the most picturesque towns in Uganda. It is the home of the President now and was the seat of British civil rule before that.

The beautifully landscaped Botanical Gardens at Entebbe.

Masaka

The old cinema in Masaka town.

On the way to Masaka, a beautifully arranged fruit and veg market, with an extraordinary vegetable balancing act.

A most dignified shopkeeper.

Sese Islands

The islands. In the early part of the century an outbreak of sleeping sickness
resulted in the evacuation of the islands, resettlement was allowed in the 1930s.
Prior to 1910 the population was about 20,000 it is now about half that.

Road grading, a very familiar sight throughout Uganda.

Three's company.

On the shores of Bugala Island.

A white pelican takes off
on Lake Victoria

An unusual fishing net.

The car ferry from Bukakata (near Masaka) to Bugala Island.
Driven by two large 100 hp engines, it still managed to run aground!

Lake Mburo National Park

Fishing boats on the shore of Lake Mburo.

One of the most beautiful birds in Uganda, the Lilac-breasted roller, *Coracias cavdata*.

Impala *Aepyceros melampus*

Perched on a throne of thorns, the magnificent African Fish Eagle *Haliaeetus vocifer*.

A male Impala, in all his glory.

A benefit of getting up for the dawn.

A small herd of Burchell's Zebra, *Hippotigris Quagga*.

The Crowned or Crested crane, *Balearica regulorum*, is the National bird of Uganda.

Yellow Billed Egrets, *Egretta Intermedia*.

A Vervet monkey,
Cercopithecus aethiops.

A female Defassa
waterbuck, *Kobus
defassa*, recognisable by
the white patch on her
rump.

Mbarara

The 'entrance' to Mbarara town.

A typical coffee shamba (small farm). The coffee bushes are often
intercropped with food crops such as bananas and casava.

Ripe coffee berries.

Harvesting coffee by hand.

Sun drying robusta coffee berries. The post harvest treatment of Robusta coffee is much simpler than Arabica; the berries are sun dried for a week or so, this makes the berry shrivel and go black and hard and becomes locally known as 'kiboko'. This is then removed by a hulling machine. By this stage the beans are ready for sale to processors who will treat them and grade them by size. Robusta coffee, because of its strong and bitter taste, is commonly used for the instant coffee market.

After hulling, the coffee beans need hand sorting. This removes any rotten beans, black beans or stones.

A coffee sack being stitched, ready for export. Each bag weighs about 60 kgs.

There are two main types of banana in Uganda; the sweet yellow ones (*musa sapientum*) eaten as fruit and matoke (pictured here) eaten when it has been cooked. Matoke is a staple food in many parts of Uganda. The banana plant has a multitude of uses; the sap of the stem used for thatching, weaving and rope making. The leaves are used in cooking (rather as Europeans use silver foil), making bedding and folded into head pads for carrying heavy loads. Matoke is generally sold by the bunch which lasts a family of six about a week. It is seen almost all over Uganda being transported by bicycle or truck.

Kabale

Kabale town was established as an administrative capital of the district
by the British in 1910. It was also one of the earliest upcountry mission stations
in Uganda. Kabale is an important trading post en route to Zaire, Rwanda
and Burundi.

A colourfully dressed boy of the local Bakiga tribe.

A view over Kigezi district.

Lake Bunyoni in Kabale district is reputed to be one of the deepest lakes
in Africa. There are no fish in the lake but it does contain a large population
of freshwater crayfish.

A Bakiga woman with her crafts at Bwama Rehabilitation Centre on Lake Bunyoni.

Bwindi Impenetrable National Park

A gorilla tracker.

The Mountain gorilla,
Gorrilla Gorilla.

The forest.

The magnificent and
awe-inspiring sight of
gorillas in their natural
environment.

Queen Elizabeth National Park

Sunrise over the Kitchwanba Escarpment.

A male baboon, *Papio cynocephalus*.

The baboon is a fierce fighter, especially when it is with its young.

The White-Browed coucal, *Centropus superciliosus*, distinguished by its creamy white eyebrow, is a carnivorous bird and is often seen foraging on the ground for small reptiles. It is a poor flyer, unable to maintain flight for more than 20 or 30 metres.

A young bull elephant, *Loxodonta africana*, ears flapping, makes a threatening gesture.

A female Cameroon bushbuck – the leg twitch is a nervous reaction.

A lioness, *Panthera leo*, in mid-hunt

Hippopotamus Amphibius.

The African buffalo, *Syncerus caffer*.

A male Uganda Kob, *Kobus Kob*.

Elephants are frequent visitors to the Kazinga Channel in the Park.

A rare clear view of the snow-capped Rwenzori Mountains across the park with
the omnipresent *Euphorbia Candelabra*.

A young Defassa waterbuck.

Jacksons Francolin,
Francolinus Jacksoni.

A foraging Wart hog,
Phacochoerus aethiopicus.

If looks could kill . . .
The Hippo is the major killer of humans in the East African region,
in areas close to water.

LEFT: Black-winged Stilt, *Himantopus himantopus*.

RIGHT: The little egret, *Egretta garzetta*, generally a solitary bird, but they sometimes congregate with other fish eaters where food is abundant.

Yellow-billed stork, *Mycteria ibis*. The slightly curved bill has given this stork its Ibis name tag. It feeds on small fish and crustaceans, using its foot to disturb the mud and shading the water with its outstretched wing.

A couple of buffaloes stay cool in the channel. The egret enjoys the ticks that congregate on the buffalo.

A yellow-billed egret, *Mesophoyx intermedius*, the friend of the buffalo.

The Saddlebill Stork, *Ephippiorhynchus senegalensis*.

The Hadada ibis, *Hagedashia hagedash*, gets its name from its raucous call. It is one of three species of ibis found in the park but unlike the others, it nests alone.

White-winged terns, *Chlidonias leucoptera*. These birds are one of the most common freshwater birds to visit Uganda from Eurasia. They do not breed here.

White-necked cormorant, *Phalacrocorax carbo*. An unusual bird in that it is equally at home in a marine environment as it is in a freshwater one.

The White Pelican, *Pelecanus onocrotalus*, on the Kazinga Channel.

The crater area.

Musicians of the Rwenzori Cultural Dancers Association playing a Bakonjo lure.

The Rukungiri Dancing Group performing a traditional Bakiga festival dance.

Katwe

A matoke selling shop.
(The more remote towns in Uganda have remained poor
because of their isolation.)

Bicycles are a common method of transport in the rural areas.

Salt crystallises on the surface of these 'salt pans' and is later collected and sold.

Packing salt into sacks on the shores of Lake Katwe. This lake is one of several explosion craters formed around 5000 BC.

The coarser and darker salt is cut from the lake bed. It is rich in minerals and is a vital component of cattle feed.

Kasese

0° near Kasese

Harvesting pineapples near Kasese. These pineapples are for the jam industry.

A Banyankole woman in traditional 'shuka' dress with her children, on their way to church.

Kasese is the town at the foot of the Rwenzori Mountains. This is Margherita Road (named after the highest peak of the mountains). Kasese was also built up as a result of British civil rule. The Indian population of Kasese was fairly high and trade was and still is very busy.

A tailor working on the corner of Margherita Road in Kasese.

A typical Ankole cow, with long thick horns and a hump on the back.

Reco's cushions, although made locally, are distributed all over Uganda.

Mattress foam before it has been cut to size.

The finished product.

Kilembe

The new and the old.
Kilembe town was built around the mines in the foothills of
the Rwenzori Mountains.

'Bats'.

Dancing at a Mothers Union meeting near Kilembe. They are wearing traditional 'gomas' dresses.

Rwenzori Mountains National Park

At the foot of the Mountains, most of the local population's main income
comes from working as porters, so they are naturally keen to get the job when
a new lot of people arrive to go up the mountains.

The Bujuku Valley is the most direct route to the heart of the Rwenzoris.
The podocarpus rain forest is characteristic of 8000–9000 feet altitude.
In the background is Mount Speke whose peak is 16,080 feet.

Looking across the lower Bigo Basin (or Bog) at 11,000 feet. The giant *Lobelia beguaeratii* are striking monuments; the one in the foreground is approximately 3 metres high. These plants, however, have a short life. In this picture only the lobelia in the foreground is living, the rest are dead. The white flowers are *Helichrysum Stuhlmannii*, the most abundant flowers in the mountains.

A giant tree groundsel.

An immature rosette of *Lobelia beguaeratii* about half a metre in diameter. They open out fully in sunlight. The young shoot that will rise from the centre is what produces the spectacular towers that characterise the Bigo Basin landscape. This species of giant lobelia is one of four relatives that occur at different altitudes.

Sunrise from Upper Bigo Bog.

Lake Bujuku is the Afro-Alpine zone at about 13,000 feet.
The giant-tree groundsel is a common feature at this altitude. Lake Bujuku is the
eastern gateway to the icy peaks. The main passes, Scott-Elliot and Stuhlman,
are approached from the south and north respectively.

A mountain stream in Kandahi Valley, fed from glacial melt water.

Porters taking a break between the Kitandara lakes.

The two Kitandara lakes viewed from the Scott-Elliot pass at 14,262 feet. In the background is Mount Luigi. On the left of the pass is the sheer face of Mount Baker and on the right is Mount Stanley, which rises to the peak called Margherita at 16,763 feet.

One of the Kitandara lakes.

Fort Portal

The necessities of life seen here in a typical general store in Fort Portal.
Much the same things can be found in shops all over Uganda.

Skilled hands.

Waiting to transport passion fruit (in the sacks) and matoke.

FACING PAGE
A waterfall near Fort Portal amongst a collection of caves called 'Mabere ga
Nyinamwiru' which means 'Caves with breasts' – a reference to the stalagmites
and stalactites in the caves.

Semliki National Park

The view across Uganda and into Zaire over the Semliki Valley. The meandering
river, the Semliki, is the border between the two countries.

The sulphurous hot springs on the road to Bundibugio. The springs are one of the rare sources of volcanic activity along the Rift Valley. Earthquakes are also common in this area.

Mubende

When he sits on the seat, due to his size, he will be unable to reach the ground,
so instead he puts one leg under the cross bar and balances without resting on any
part of the bike.

Luwero

A bicycle repair and spares shop. A crate of components has just been unloaded
and they are assembling the bicycles to sell.

Masindi

Harvesting papyrus stems. These stems are carefully dried and are used for
thatching and mat-making.

School children on parade near Masindi.

Murchison Falls National Park

The top of Murchison
Falls where the Victoria
Nile is forced through a
6-metre gap in the rocks.

The falls from the bottom. Here you can see the narrow gap through which the Nile is forced.

There are two distinct falls; Baker had noticed both but later visitors found that the northern falls were seasonal. During 1961 and 1962, there was an exceptional rainfall and the force of the river opened the second falls permanently. The park suffered incredible damage. Most of the roads had to be relocated and virtually all the National Parks flotilla was washed away.

Jackson's hartebeeste, *Alcelaphus buselaphus jacksoni*, was named after Sir Frederick
Jackson who gave a particularly memorable talk on the animal to the Royal
Geographical Society in 1891. It is one of the fastest antelopes in Africa.

The Borassus palm. A common tree in the park, its fruits being a particular favourite with elephants, it has spread around the park via their droppings.

A view across the plains of Murchison.

The elegant Rothschild's giraffe, *Giraffa cameloparadalis rothschildi*. The largest concentration of these animals in Uganda is in the northern sector of this park.

African buffaloes, still very shy.

The African Rock python. The largest snake in Africa and very rarely seen in the water.

A pair of Ruppell's vultures, *Gyps ruppellis*.

Sunset from the top of the Falls, looking down the Nile.

Nebbi

A Jonam woman carrying thatching grass.

The Arua to Kampala bus stops in Nebbi and is swarmed by street vendors selling
supplies for the journey

Arua

Swaib Alli, a *mzee* (old man) of the Acholi tribe.

Main Street, Arua.
The climate is different
in the north of Uganda.
It is considerably hotter
and dryer than the rest of
the country.

A typical Kakwa
homestead near Arua.
The smaller hut is used
for grain storage mainly
but occasionally for
meat.

Moyo

Moyo town.

Laropi

The River Nile provides all the necessary facilities for these women.

Gulu

The main junction in Gulu, northern Uganda.

The Acholi Inn, found in Gulu. This hotel is one of Uganda Hotels chain, which
has hotels in almost every town in Uganda.

OVERLEAF
An Acholi woman. The Acholi are a Nilo-Hamitic tribe covering
the central northern area.

Lugazi

Together with sugar, tea is the only crop grown in large estates in Uganda. Tea was
first introduced from India and Ceylon in the early 1900s by the British. It was not
until just before the Second World War that tea was exported in any quantity.

Harvesting the tea is done by hand. It is a laborious yet skilled task as only certain leaves can be picked.

After the day's collection, the leaves are taken to the factory for treatment.

The drying beds in the tea factory. The tea leaves are put here first and left for a preliminary drying period.

One of the many machines in a tea factory, the Rotor Vane machine crushes and shreds the tea leaves.

Seeta

The first stage in brickmaking; digging up and moistening the clay.

A large kiln is made up of about 3,000 bricks. A fire is built in the centre and is stoked for at least 24 hours. After baking, the bricks are ready to be used.

Storage of the finished product. The grass is used to prevent rain damage.

Jinja

Owen Falls Dam, built in
1954, supplies most of
Uganda's electricity.

The original site discovered by Speke as the source of the Nile. Formerly Rippon Falls, the falls and the original plaque were buried when the river was dammed.

Bujugali Falls, just a few minutes drive from Jinja.

A street cobbler in Jinja.

The seamstress.

Main Street, Jinja looking deserted on a Sunday morning. Jinja was first established as a settlement by the Imperial British East Africa Company in the early 1890s because of its significant location on the lake. It became a town when Sir Gerald Portal moved the civil headquarters for Busoga from Iganga to Jinja.

This huge pile of scrap metal will be melted down and made into steel bars,
which will then go on to become anything from pots and pans to car bodies.

Slag cutting.
This makes the large pieces of slag into manageable pieces.

The Electric Arc Furnace. This is where the scrap is dumped and melted. Here the top is off the furnace in preparation for a load of scrap.

'Tapping' the Electric Arc Furnace. This process involves the whole furnace tilting downwards and the fully molten steel pours out into a large ladle from where it is poured into the clay moulds.

Action on the cooling bed. The red hot strips of rolled steel come out of the
rollers, are picked up by a worker with heavy tongs and dragged onto the cooling
bed, where they are left to cool down.

Sunrise over the Kakira sugar plantation, near Jinja.
The dawn for this plantation was 1929.

Endless fields of sugar cane. Uganda used to be self-sufficient in sugar production with a large surplus for export. The Asian exodus of 1972 was responsible for the collapse of the sugar industry. The industry is beginning to recover but faces stiff competition from imported sugar.

The cane is still harvested by hand.

Loading the harvested cane, to be taken to the factory.

Off-loading the harvested cane into the sugar factory.

Inside the sugar factory.

Bagging the sugar.

Tororo

The granite monolith that is Tororo Rock.

On the way into Tororo town.

Mbale

Sunset over the Teso plains in Mbale district.

Republic Street, Mbale. This town was founded in 1902 as the administrative capital of the region by the British. They appointed Semei Kakungulu as King. Mbale was then a very desolate place, but was chosen because of its proximity to a large grove of matoke.

The top of Sipi Falls.

The bottom of Sipi Falls.
These more gentle
waterfalls are located in
the east of Uganda on
Mount Elgon, near the
village of Sipi.

Sunset from Mount Elgon with Moroto Hill in Southern Karamoja
in the far distance.

Hand pulping a days pickings on Mount Elgon. Red-ripe Arabica berries are picked from the bushes, at the end of the day the skin and soft pulp around the beans are left to soak in clean water overnight. This process softens the hard parchment immediately around the beans thus facilitating the hand cleaning. The coffee is then dried and sold as 'parchment' coffee. The 'pulp' of the coffee berry is very acidic and must be removed within 24 hours of picking to avoid the coffee bean being affected. The flavour of Arabica coffee (grown in the highlands) is milder than Robusta (grown in the lowlands) and the bean needs the washing process to keep its flavour and price.

Kapchorwa

One of the fruit vendors in the small market town.

A trader in Kapchorwa town. Second-hand clothes are big business in Uganda.
Generally imported by a handful of wealthy traders in Kampala, they are sold by
the bale and find their way to every corner of the country.

The pharmacist.

The main street of
Kapchorwa town.

Kaabong

A Karimojong village near Kaabong. These villages are made up of mud and clay
huts with thatch roofs completely surrounded by a large fence, made from bush,
scrub and sticks. The villages are frequently circular in shape.

An unmarried Karimojong woman, near Kaabong. The cicatrices on the chest and
forehead are very typical of the Nilo-Hamitic tribes.

The main street of Kaabong in the heart of Karamoja.

Karimojong men outside their village.

Kidepo Valley National Park

Looking across the Narus Valley.
The Narus Valley, despite the apparent dryness seen here, is the parks' only year
round water supply. Consequently, many different animals can be seen in a
relatively small area during the dry season. It was also a traditional seasonal
gathering place for many tribes in Uganda, Sudan and Kenya who used
to come here to hunt.

A small herd of African buffalo.
When in large numbers these animals are easily spooked.

A few Burchell's zebra looking for precious green shoots. These animals are common throughout the park.

The Eland, *Tragelaphus oryx*, is Uganda's largest antelope.

Rothschild's giraffe is the only species of giraffe found in Uganda.
There are very few surviving in this park.

A herd of elephants in the Narus Valley.